TM

COLLECTAFACT

WORDS AND PICTURES   **THAT WORK TOGETHER**

VIKINGS

TM

LONDON · PRINCETON

What's in the book

*All words in the text which appear in **bold** can be found in the glossary*

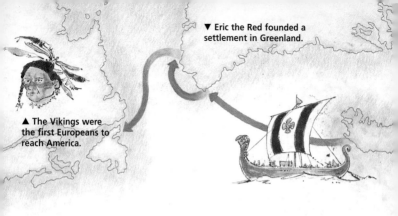

▼ Eric the Red founded a settlement in Greenland.

▲ The Vikings were the first Europeans to reach America.

"on 8 June the ravages of heathen men miserably destroyed God's church on Lindisfarne with plunder and slaughter…"
(Anglo-Saxon Chronicle, AD 793)

▶ Lindisfarne was an island whose wealthy, unprotected monastery was an easy target for the Vikings.

The Viking world

The first glimpse many European people had of the Vikings was when the Viking **longships** appeared off their coasts. No-one was prepared for the invading warriors and few countries could resist the Vikings. From the first attacks in AD 787, Viking raids were a frequent occurrence all over northwestern Europe for the next 200 years.

FastFact
The Vikings called North America Vinland, which means Land of Wine.

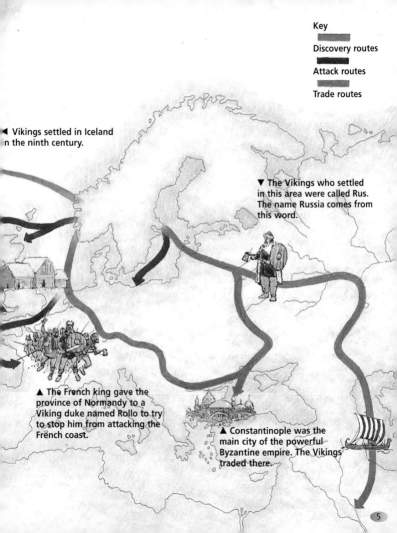

Key

Discovery routes

Attack routes

Trade routes

◀ Vikings settled in Iceland in the ninth century.

▼ The Vikings who settled in this area were called Rus. The name Russia comes from this word.

▲ The French king gave the province of Normandy to a Viking duke named Rollo to try to stop him from attacking the French coast.

▲ Constantinople was the main city of the powerful Byzantine empire. The Vikings traded there.

Viking lands

Vikings came from the north European countries that are now called Sweden, Norway and Denmark. These lands are cold and bleak, with deep **rivers**, rocky coasts and towering mountains. Even though the Vikings fished and hunted wild animals, there was not enough land to produce food for all of them.

Many Vikings sought a better life by using their skills as seamen and warriors.

Viking lands were divided into several kingdoms. The richest, most powerful men became leaders such as kings and dukes.

These leaders would call the **free men** to a meeting called the **Althing**, where they would discuss plans about expeditions to other countries or make decisions about local problems. Often, there were wars between the kingdoms, particularly over pieces of good land.

▲ Men gathering for the Althing.

◀ The narrow, deep-watered fjords of Scandinavia form perfect natural harbours.

FastFact
Many places in Britain are named by the Vikings, for example, Thorsby is named after the god, Thor.

Pirates or traders?

Pirates

The Vikings attacked the lands around them, particularly Britain and France. They stole food and treasures and carried people away to become **slaves**. People who lived in isolated areas on the coast or on **islands** were terrified of Viking attacks. They were mostly farmers and were not used to defending themselves and their families. They added to their daily prayers the words: "God deliver us from the fury of the Northmen."

▲ Viking helmets like this one have been found at a number of gravesites in Europe. Soldiers were often buried with all their weapons because the Vikings believed they would need them in the afterlife.

▼ Rope was wrapped around the hilt of Viking swords to make them easier to grip.

Traders

In certain places, the Vikings got food and goods by trading rather than by attacking and stealing. This was usually when the inhabitants were stronger and could defend themselves. Vikings travelled as far as the Black Sea, trading their furs, jewellery and slaves for spices and wine.

▶ Goods were sold for a weight, rather than for a number, of gold or silver coins. When the Vikings needed change, they simply broke a coin in half!

FastFact
Contrary to popular belief, the Vikings did not have horns on their helmets!

9

Longships

The Vikings were superb sailors and they used ships for travelling on the **lakes**, seas and **fjords** of **Scandinavia** – as well as for trips further away from home. The ships were measured by the number of **oars** they had. The smallest, a **faering**, had four oars, and the largest, a **longship**, had about 32. The oars were used on inland waters when there wasn't enough wind to fill the sail.

A big longship could be up to 30m long and would travel at up to 32km/h under full sail. Ships were so important to the Vikings that their language contained dozens of different ways of saying 'ship'.

The Vikings could **navigate** by watching the stars and the Sun, as well as by using familiar landmarks such as **islands** and mountains. They also looked out for birds found in different places at different times of the year, such as puffins and fulmars.

▲ Viking ships were among the first to have a keel, which helped them to sail very fast through water and made them stable even in rough weather

▶ Oars were used if the sail was not up, when there was no wind or on inland waters. Each rower kept his belongings and a waterproof reindeer-skin sleeping bag with him on the boat.

▶ The gaps between the oak planks of the ship were made waterproof by filling them with sheep's wool dipped in tar.

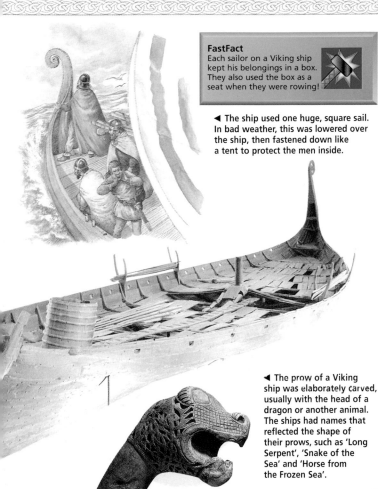

◀ The ship used one huge, square sail. In bad weather, this was lowered over the ship, then fastened down like a tent to protect the men inside.

◀ The prow of a Viking ship was elaborately carved, usually with the head of a dragon or another animal. The ships had names that reflected the shape of their prows, such as 'Long Serpent', 'Snake of the Sea' and 'Horse from the Frozen Sea'.

Heroes

The Vikings admired bold and fearless men such as soldiers, sailors and explorers. The deeds of these heroes were told so often that they became more like myths than historical fact.

Leif Ericson

The first people to sail from Europe to North America were Vikings! In AD 1002, an expedition led by Leif Ericson landed on the coast of what is now the USA. The Vikings named the country Vinland and built a village. After three years in America, the Vikings were attacked by Native Americans and left soon afterwards.

King Cnut

In 1016, a Viking from Denmark named Cnut, son of the chieftain, Sweyn Forkbeard, became the king of England. He was a wise ruler who brought peace and stability.

Harald Haardraade

The Byzantine emperor used an elite fighting force of Vikings called the **Varangarian Guard**. Harald Haardraade, or Hard-nose, was a famous member, and later became king of Norway.

He was the last Viking leader to land with an army in England.

Sagas and runes

Viking children did not go to school. Instead, lessons came in the form of long stories, or **sagas**. These described the adventures of the gods or of great Viking warriors. The stories were important ways of teaching history, geography and **navigation**. The Vikings decorated some buildings with pictures from famous sagas.

▲ This wood carving shows Sigurd the Dragon-Slayer attacking a dragon.

This stone carving shows one of the tales of Odin, the Vikings' god of war. You can see Odin in the centre at the top, handing a sword to an old man.

The Futhark

The Viking alphabet was called the **futhark**. The letters, or **runes**, were formed mainly by straight lines which were usually carved into wood or stone.

FastFact
In Norse myth the **Valkyries** rushed into a battle and picked out the most heroic from among the dead.

a	b	c	d		e	f	g	h

ij	k	l	m		n	o	p	q

r	s	t	uvw		x	y	z

The Viking gods

The Vikings believed there were lots of gods who lived in a place called **Asgard**. Each god was responsible for a different thing, such as war, travel or the home. These gods were not perfect. They had very human qualities including weaknesses, such as jealousy and greed.

If a Viking died in battle, he was thought to go to a hall in Asgard called **Valhalla**, where everybody fought all day and feasted all night.

Some Important Gods

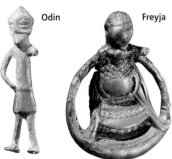

Odin   Freyja   Thor

THOR, the god of thunder, was the most popular god. He had a quick temper but was very good-hearted.

FREY made sure that the Sun shone, the rain fell and the crops grew. He had a magic boat which he kept folded up in his pocket.

FREYJA was Frey's sister and was the goddess of love. Freyja could turn herself into a bird.

ODIN, or Woden, was the god of war, who rode an eight-legged horse.

LOKI was half god, half fire-spirit. He caused the other gods a lot of trouble.

FastFact
Odin was master of magic and discovered the **runes**, the letters of the Viking alphabet.

▲ When Viking warriors died, their bodies were often put in longships, which were then buried or set on fire and pushed out to sea.

▶ By the end of the Viking age, the Vikings were turning to Christianity. This 11th-century mould was used to make crosses and copies of Mjollnir, Thor's hammer.

A Viking village

When they were not raiding or trading, the warriors returned to their villages. The villages were lively, bustling places with lots of people working and playing in different areas. The men may have gone off hunting, leaving the women to rear the children and work the farm, just as they did when the men were away.

Raiding
Prisoners captured by the Vikings on raids on foreign lands were brought back to the village to work as slav

Hunting
Vikings hunted many animals including seals, whales, wild boar, deer, elk and even polar bears. As well as food, these animals provided fur for warm clothing, feathers for soft bedding and bone, used for carving combs and other items.

Marriages
In Viking times, marriages were usually arranged by parents. Men were allowed more than one wife and having lots of wives was considered a sign of importance and wealth. The husband was always the head of the family. At meal times he sat in a special chair while the rest of the family sat on benches. Viking wives were expected to obey their husbands, but they had more rights than other women at the time. Viking women were allowed to own property and share their husbands' wealth. And if they got fed up with their husbands they could get a divorce whenever they liked!

Farming
Most Vikings were **bondi**, or farmers, not warriors. They grew **cereals** and vegetables, including peas, beans, turnips, onions and cabbage, and raised **livestock**. Vikings also fished for cod, herring and salmon and hunted wild animals for food.

Ships and boats

The Vikings were the first ship builders to put a **keel** on their boats. This helped to stop the boat rolling from side to side, making it faster, more stable and easier to steer. **Longships**, used for battle and warfare, were up to 30m in length and took 60 oarsmen to row them. Merchant ships, called **knorrs**, were 15m long and were used to carry goods for trading. Small boats, called **faerings**, had just four oars and were used for short journeys.

Ravens

A flag with a raven on it was often flown on Viking ships. Ravens were kept on board the ships because the sailors believed they were good at finding land. If the ship got lost at sea, the sailors would release a raven and watch which way it flew off. Then they would sail in that direction.

Fjords

Viking settlements were almost always built on the banks of a **river** or a **fjord**. The coast of Scandinavian countries has many fjords along it. This meant that Vikings could travel from one village to another very easily by boat.

Housing

Viking houses were usually just one storey high. The walls were made of stone or wood and the roof was either thatched or covered in turf. There were no windows in Viking houses – which made them pretty gloomy places! Inside every home was a large open fireplace, used to cook food and provide heat and light. Usually an entire family including grandparents, aunts and uncles lived under one roof. Vikings ate two meals a day – one in the morning and one in the evening. They used knives and spoons (but not forks) and drank out of cups made from animal horns.

At home

The Vikings were not only skilled soldiers and seafarers but also farmers who lived with their families, growing and making everything they needed. Children helped with the chores as soon as they were able. Even very small children had their own jobs, such as feeding the animals or gathering firewood.

Viking women worked on the farm and wove material for clothes and blankets on small looms. When their husbands were away fighting or exploring, the women took care of the whole farm.

Viking houses were made of timber and woven branches, with turf or thatched roofs Where there was no wood, such as in Shetland and Iceland, stone was used. Inside, the houses were divided into rooms by stretching cloth or skins between the pillars that supported the roof.

A typical farm had a house where all the members of the family lived together. There were also sheds for the animals, a workshop for making metal tools and small huts for slaves.

Hygiene

● Viking homes were not as clean as our houses are. Bones and vegetable scraps were left on the floor in winter and only cleared out in the spring.
● In spring, rubbish was buried outside.
● Vikings often suffered from head lice, so most people had combs.

Games

Children had some time to play games and carve wooden toys. In winter, they skated using carved bone as blades, which they strapped to their shoes with leather.

On dark, cold evenings, Viking children may have played a game called **hnefatafl**, which was similar to chess.

FastFact
By AD 886, the Vikings ruled a very large area of northeast England.

Crafts

Vikings were very skilled craftsmen, making objects from stone, wood and metal. Many of the most beautiful objects were not made by artists, but by ordinary people. A farmer might make a brooch using the same furnace he used to make his plough.

Professional people wore their wealth in the form of jewellery. This was the best way to keep it safe as there were no banks.

Blacksmiths were highly respected. Thor, one of the important Viking gods, used a smith's hammer as his main weapon.

▲ Some jewellery was made especially to be buried with a dead person. This 'arm-ring' was found at a burial site.

Make Viking Jewellery

Look at the decoration on the Viking objects in this book. Can you see how all the figures are woven around each other? The Vikings loved to use complicated patterns for decoration. Try making a bracelet or brooch from modelling clay using Viking designs.

◀ Use small balls of clay to make the shapes of the heads below.

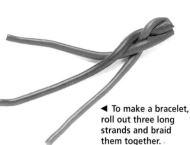

◀ To make a bracelet, roll out three long strands and braid them together.

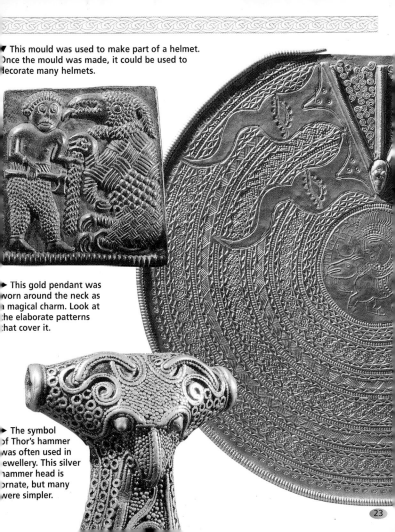

▼ This mould was used to make part of a helmet. Once the mould was made, it could be used to decorate many helmets.

► This gold pendant was worn around the neck as a magical charm. Look at the elaborate patterns that cover it.

► The symbol of Thor's hammer was often used in jewellery. This silver hammer head is ornate, but many were simpler.

Food and drink

Finding food was an important part of the Vikings' lives. Very little land was fertile and the winters were long and harsh. The Vikings ate rich stews of beef, mutton, fish or whale meat. They also grew vegetables, such as peas, cabbage, beans, wild leeks and garlic.

Tables were set up for meals and family members would sit on the same wooden benches that they slept on at night. They ate from rectangular wooden platters or soapstone bowls, using spoons and knives that they carried on their belts.

The Vikings used drinking horns as well as cups. The horns did not have flat bottoms, so they were passed around the table from person to person until they were empty. Anyone who could empty a drinking horn in one turn was admired. The usual drink was mead, a sweet beer made from honey.

Food Facts

- The Vikings used peas to make bread when they had no grain.
- Salt was made by boiling sea water.
- The Vikings ate two meals a day: the day meal after the early farm work and the night meal at the end of the day.

▼ Cooking was done over an open hearth fire. Meat was roasted on huge spits and stews were made in big iron cauldrons. Sometimes a gridiron, made of coiled iron as shown below, was used. It was heated in a fire then placed underneath a cooking pot. Does it remind you of any part of a modern stove?

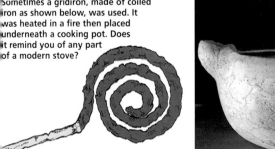

▼ Bowls were made from pottery or from a substance called soapstone.

Clothes

Most Viking clothes were made from coarse woollen cloth, although some rich people wore imported silk or linen. In winter, people wore furs to keep warm.

Men wore undershirts, breeches, long, woollen trousers and long tunics. Around their waists they wore a leather belt which carried purses, spoons and knives.

Women wore wool or linen dresses with a tunic that looked like an apron and was attached with brooches.

▲ Shoes were made from leather or goatskin, laced up with strips of leather.

Thor visits the land of the giants

This story is part of a Viking saga. It is about Thor, the god of thunder, and the journey on which he set out to prove his strength. His journey and trials of strength would have been very familiar to the Vikings.

One day, Thor, Loki and their two servants set off to visit Utgard, land of the giants. After a long journey, they arrived at the gates of Utgard to find them locked.

Thor hammered on the gates, calling for someone to come and let them in, but Loki slipped through the bars, dragging the others after him. They walked into the great hall of Utgard. In the middle was a long table around which hundreds of giants sat on benches eating and drinking. The giants all began to laugh as Thor marched up to the Giant King seated at the end of the hall.

"Greetings, Giant King," said Thor.

The king sat chewing bones and ignored Thor. From time to time, he tossed a bone over his shoulder and picked up a new one.

Thor spoke again, this time a little louder: "Greetings, Gi–"

The Giant King interrupted: "So, you're the great thunder god, Thor, are you? Well, you look awfully scrawny to me. I suppose you've come to test your strength?"

Thor was furious at the Giant King's rudeness but he did not want to lose his temper when he was surrounded by giants.

"What skill would you like to challenge us with?" continued the Giant King.

Thor looked at the giants around him.

"I doubt if anyone here can drink as much as I can," Thor replied.

The Giant King signalled to a servant, who brought forward a huge drinking horn.

"This is used by my followers," he said.

"A good drinker can finish it in one try. Let us see what the great Thor can do!"

Thor took the horn, raised it to his mouth and began to swallow. He felt sure he could drink it all, but he ran out of breath and found that it was no less full than before. He drank a second time and this time the horn was no longer brimming full. He drank a third time, but although the level was lower than before, the horn was by no means empty.

"You don't seem to be much of a drinker," said the Giant King. "Why not try your strength? The younger giants like to test themselves by lifting my cat. We don't think this much of a feat, but perhaps you'd like to try?"

Standing beside the Giant King's chair was the most enormous cat Thor had ever seen. He braced himself and then put both arms under the cat and heaved. The cat simply arched its back. Thor heaved again and managed to make the cat lift one paw off the ground before he had to admit defeat.

"As I thought," said the Giant King. "You may be strong in Asgard and in the realms of men, but your strength is nothing here."

Thor grew angry at this. "I can match any of your men in a fight. Just let anyone here wrestle with me."

There was a roar of laughter from all the giants in the hall.

"Everyone here feels that wrestling with you would be too easy," said the Giant King.

"But, you could fight Elli, my foster mother."

A wrinkled old woman hobbled forward. Thor thought that the Giant King was making fun of him – until Elli took hold of him. Then he knew that his strength would be sorely tested. They struggled and fought, but eventually Elli threw Thor off balance and he landed on one knee.

"Enough, enough!" shouted the Giant King. "You have shown us that you are no wrestler. You pose no threat, so you may eat with us and spend the night here."

Thor and his companions were hungry and tired after their long journey. When they had eaten, they spread their bedding in a space on the floor among the giants. Thor awoke early, before any of the giants, and roused his companions.

"Come, let's go before the giants wake up," he whispered.

Thor, Loki and their two servants tiptoed over the sleeping giants and all the way out of the gates of Utgard. To their surprise, they found the Giant King already outside

waiting for them. He walked with them across the plain for a while. He finally stopped and said: "This is where I must leave you. Thor, do not feel upset about your failures last night." Thor was puzzled.

"But I have never before been so badly beaten," he said.

The Giant King replied: "You were not competing in a fair fight. I feared your strength, so I used magic to deceive you. The other end of the horn that you drank from was in the sea. When you reach the shore you will see just how much you have lowered its level. The cat you lifted was really the giant serpent whose body is wrapped around the world. You managed to lift it until its back touched the sky. And as for Elli, it was a wonder you withstood her for so long. You see, Elli is Old Age, which defeats all men in time."

Thor was furious that he had been tricked. He seized his hammer and swung it around, but the Giant King and Utgard had vanished, as if they had never been there.

How we know

Have you ever wondered how, although the Vikings lived over 1,000 years ago, we know so much about their daily lives?

Evidence from the Ground

Many Viking objects have been preserved in the ground. They are often ordinary things that may have been thrown away by the Vikings because they were broken or no longer needed. By carefully piecing them back together, **archaeologists** can work out what they are and how the Vikings used them.

Evidence Around Us

Many places in Europe were originally given Viking names, and so we can tell where they settled. The whole of Normandy in France was taken over by the Vikings, and the name means 'land of the Northmen'. In Britain, many place names have the Viking endings '-thorpe' and '-by', including Scunthorpe and Grimsby.

And did you know that Wednesday was originally Woden's day and that Thursday was called Thor's day?

Evidence from Books

Many of the stories told by the Vikings were written down, and so it is easy to find out who the important gods were and what various historical figures did. We even know that when Eric the Red discovered Greenland, he gave it that name in spite of its cold iciness because "many would want to go there if it had so promising a name".

Glossary

Afterlife The life that begins after death.

Althing A council of free men that met when problems arose in their country. It was the only form of government the Vikings had.

Archaeologist Someone who studies human history by uncovering ancient objects and physical remains.

Asgard In Viking belief this is where their gods lived and where they themselves would go when they died.

Bondi Viking farmers.

Byzantine empire An empire centred around Byzantium (now called Istanbul). It was the strongest world power at the time of the Vikings and lasted from the 6th to the 15th century.

Cereals Crops such as barley, oats and rye.

Clinker built Made out of overlapping planks of wood.

Day meal The first meal of the day. It was eaten after the early farm work had been done.

Faering The smallest type of Viking ship. It had four oars and was used for short journeys.

Fjord (pronounced 'fee-ord') is a long, narrow body of water that stretches inland from the sea.

Free men Men who were not slaves.

Futhark The runic alphabet used by the Vikings. The word is taken from the sounds of the first six letters.

Gridiron A coiled metal strip which was placed in the fire and used to heat pots.

Hnefatafl A board game played by the Vikings.

Hull The underside of a ship.

Inlet An area of water that stretches into the land.

Island An area of land that is completely surrounded by water.

Jarl A Viking leader or lord.

Keel The long piece of wood that forms the lowest part of a ship and helps it to balance.

Knorr A type of Viking ship used for trading.

Lake A large body of water surrounded by land.

Livestock Animals that are kept by farmers, such as cattle, sheep, goats, pigs and chickens. They are used to make money from their milk, coats, meat, and other products.

Longship The long, low ship used by the Vikings.

Mjollnir Thor's hammer. He carried it with him at all times.

Monastery A place where monks live. Monasteries often contain valuable items, such as jewellery.

Navigate To navigate a ship is to sail it in a particular direction.

Night meal The meal eaten by the Vikings after all the work was done, when it began to get dark.

Northmen The name given to the Vikings by the people they attacked or traded with. 'Viking' was a term they used to describe themselves.

Oar A pole with a wide, flat end, used for rowing or steering a boat by pushing it against the water.

Pendant A piece of jewellery that hangs from a cord or chain.

Prow The front end of a ship.

Reeve An official who lived in an English village and was loyal to the king.

River A large amount of water flowing over land to the sea or to a lake. A river carves a channel for itself in the land.

Rune A letter of the Viking alphabet which was made up of straight lines so that it could be carved in wood or stone.

Saga A story about the adventures of gods or heroes. Sagas were usually passed on by word of mouth, but some were written.

Scandinavia The group of countries from which the Vikings originated. They include Denmark, Norway, Sweden and Iceland.

slave A person who was legally owned by another person in Viking times. Slavery is now illegal in all countries.

starboard The right-hand side of a boat or ship.

stern The rear end of a boat or ship.

Valhalla The hall in Asgard where Viking warriors hoped to go when they died. In Valhalla, they could fight all day and feast all night.

Valkyries The handmaidens of Odin in Norse myth. In Valhalla, the Valkyries served the heroes with mead and ale in the skulls of those they had beaten in battle.

Varangarian Guard A section of the Byzantine army made up of Vikings. The Varangarian Guard was the emperor's bodyguard.

Work book

Work book

Rules of Hnefatafl

Hnefatafl was one of the Vikings' favourite games. The game is based on a Viking raid, and the rules are easy to learn. Make a copy of the board below and the pieces (one king, 12 defending soldiers and 20 attackers). Then all you need is someone to play against!

- There are two armies – attackers and defenders.

- The attacking army's pieces are blue and the defender's pieces are white.

- The attacker's army is trying to trap the king so that he cannot move.

- Once the king is trapped, the attackers have won and the game is over.

- The defender's army is trying to help the king escape to safety.

- To win the game, the defender's king must get to one of the green squares in any of the four corners.

▲ At the start of the game, the king is on the central square, surrounded by his defending army. The attacking army is lined up along the four edges of the board.

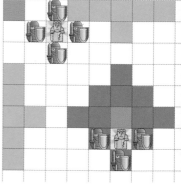

▲ The attacking army's pieces can trap and capture the king by surrounding him on all four sides or on just three sides against the central square.

- Players take turns, moving one piece at a time.

- All the pieces on the board move in exactly the same way.

- All the pieces move in straight lines: up and down or from side to side.

- You can move a piece as many squares as you like. But you are not allowed to jump other pieces.

- Pieces are not able to land on a square if it is already occupied by another piece.

- All pieces can jump across the square in the middle as long as the king is not on it!

- The king's squares are the green ones in each corner and the central square. Only the king can land on one of the king's squares.

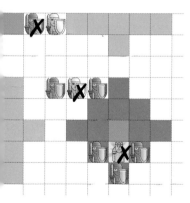

▲ Any piece can be captured when trapped between two of its opponent's pieces or between the corner squares and an opponent's piece.

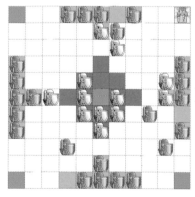

▲ Finally, the defender's king wins the game by avoiding capture and landing on one of the green squares at any of the four corners of the board.

Design your own longship

Questions and answers

There are probably lots of questions you would like to ask about the Vikings and their way of life. Squawk the Raven certainly has a few. And if you want to learn about Viking warriors, then Dan the Dane is your man with all the answers!

Why did the Vikings raid other lands?
Vikings came from Northern Europe where good farmland was hard to find. As the population grew, villages got overcrowded and they could not produce enough food. Neighbouring villages raided one another. So Vikings set sail in search of richer rewards.

For a Viking there was no greater honour than to die in battle and so they fought with great courage. The fiercest fighters became heroes and sagas were told of their brave deeds on the battlefield.

Dan the Dane

When did the Viking raids begin?
The first Viking raid on England was in AD 787. Three Viking ships sailed from Denmark and landed on the Dorset coast in England. The local **reeve** welcomed them, thinking they were friendly traders. Instead they drew their swords and killed him!

What did the Vikings steal?
They plundered churches and monasteries for their gold, stole food from farms and took prisoners to use as **slaves**. They returned home rich men and were hailed as heroes by the Viking villagers.

What were the raiders' tactics?
Viking ships could be rowed right up to the beach. Before the locals had time to raise the alarm, the warriors were ashore and charging towards them. Once all the defenders had been killed or captured, the Vikings gathered up the loot, then they burned the rest of the village to the ground.

What were Viking swords like?
Viking swords had a broad blade that was sharp on both edges. Swords would often be engraved with ornate designs and handed down from father to son as treasured family heirlooms. Some Vikings were so fond of their swords that they gave them names, like 'Gold-blade' or 'Head-splitter'.

What other weapons did the Vikings have?
The most popular Viking weapon was the broad axe. This was a long-handled axe with

a large, flat blade. It was so big a warrior had to use two hands to swing it! Other Viking weapons included bows and arrows, spears and daggers.

What did Vikings wear in battle?
Viking leaders, called **Jarls**, wore metal helmets but most helmets were made of leather. Warriors also carried a round wooden shield and wore protective clothing made from layers of tough animal hide strengthened with pieces of bone.

How did the Vikings get their name?
The word 'vik' in the Viking language, Old Norse, meant an **inlet** to the sea. Most Viking villages were built along the banks of viks. So Vikings meant the people who lived next to viks. Over time, the word Viking came to mean a pirate or raider.

What did other people call them?
In England, they were known as Northmen because they came from countries in the north of Europe. Northmen was also written as Norsemen. Today, people still use the word Norse as another word for Viking.

Did Viking warriors settle in other countries?
Many Vikings settled in the villages that they raided. More and more villages came under Viking control and soon they were in charge of large parts of other countries. By AD 911, Vikings ruled an area of France. It was called Normandy because it was the home of the Northmen.

Squawk is a raven. Her name comes from the loud noise she makes when she wants attention.

Squawk the Raven

What did the god Odin have power over?
Odin was the god of war, poetry, wisdom and agriculture. The Anglo-Saxons called him Woden. For Vikings, the most binding of all promises was called 'the promise of Odin'. When Vikings made this promise, they passed their hand through a huge silver ring kept especially for this purpose.

What objects were most important to Thor?
Thor's three most important possessions were a hammer, iron gloves and a magic belt. The hammer symbolised thunder and lightning, the iron gloves helped Thor to throw the hammer, and the magic belt doubled the Viking god's strength.

Did the Norse gods wear jewellery?
In Norse myth, Freyja, the goddess of love, always wore a necklace called *Brisingamen* and because of this, she was often called 'ornament-loving'. Thor wore his magic belt and Frey, the Sun god, kept a magic boat folded up in his pocket.

Index

www.two-canpublishing.com

Published by Two-Can Publishing
43–45 Dorset Street,
London W1U 7NA

© Two-Can Publishing 2001, 1997

For information on Two-Can books and multimedia,
call (0)20 7224 2440, fax (0)20 7224 7005, or visit our
website at http://www.two-canpublishing.com

Created by
act-two
346 Old Street
London EC1V 9RB

'Two-Can' is a trademark of Two-Can Publishing.
Two-Can Publishing is a division of
Zenith Entertainment Ltd,
43–45 Dorset Street, London W1U 7NA.

ISBN 1–85434–924–4

2 4 6 8 10 9 7 5 3 1

A catalogue record for this book is
available from the British Library

Photograph credits: Werner Forman Archives: front cover,
pp.6–13, p.16, p.17, p.22 (t), p.23, p.25, p.32 (t), p.33 (b);
Toby Maudsley: p.22 (b), p.24; Ronald Sheridan: p.32 (c);
York Archaeological Trust: p.21, p.26
Illustration credits: Kevin Maddison: pp.2–3 p.9, p.11
pp.12–13, p.14, p.17, pp.20–21, pp24–25, p.26; Maxine
Hamil: pp.27–35; James Jarvis, Carlo Tartaglia, Jeffrey Lewis
John Richardson and Dai Owen:pp.18–19, 44–45

Every effort has been made to acknowledge correctly and
contact the source of each picture and Two-Can Publishing
apologises for any unintentional errors or omissions which
will be corrected in future editions of this book.

Printed in Hong Kong by Wing King Tong